# THE ADOPTION PAPERS

**Jackie Kay** was born in 1961 in Edinburgh and brought up in Glasgow. She won an Eric Gregory Award for *The Adoption Papers* in 1991. Her first play, *Chiaroscuro*, was presented by Theatre of Black Women in 1986, and her second, *Twice Over*, by Gay Sweatshop in 1988. Her television work includes films on pornography, AIDS and transracial adoption, and *Twice through the Heart*, a poetry documentary for BBC 2. She lives in London.

# THE ADOPTION
# PAPERS

## Jackie Kay

*Oct 1992*

*For Beryl!*
*all good wishes*

*Jackie Kay*

BLOODAXE BOOKS

ISBN: 1 85224 156 X

First published 1991 by
Bloodaxe Books Ltd,
P.O. Box 1SN,
Newcastle upon Tyne NE99 1SN.

Second impression 1992.

Bloodaxe Books Ltd acknowledges
the financial assistance of Northern Arts.

Cover reproduction by V & H Reprographics, Newcastle upon Tyne.

Cover printing by J. Thomson Colour Printers Ltd, Glasgow.

Printed in Great Britain by
Bell & Bain Limited, Glasgow, Scotland.

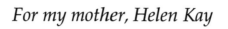

*For my mother, Helen Kay*

# Acknowledgements

A dramatisation of *The Adoption Papers* was broadcast in BBC Radio 3's *Drama Now* series in August 1990. Poems from this book have also been broadcast on *The Bandung File* (Channel 4), *Wordworks* (Tyne Tees Television), *New Voices* (BBC Radio 3), *Kaleidoscope* and *Time for Verse* (BBC Radio 4), and on the Open University programme *Literature in the Modern World* (BBC 2). Some of these poems were included in a collection for which Jackie Kay won an Eric Gregory Award in 1991, and some in a pamphlet, *That Distance Apart* (Turret Books, 1991).

Acknowledgements are also due to the editors of the following publications in which some of these poems first appeared: *Beautiful Barbarians* (Onlywomen Press, 1986), *Bête Noire, The Black Scholar* (USA), *Black Women Talk Poetry* (Black Womentalk, 1987), *Chapman, City Limits, Conditions* (USA), *Critical Quarterly, Faces in a Crowd* (Viking, 1990), *Feminist Review, The New British Poetry* (Paladin, 1988), *New Women Poets* (Bloodaxe, 1990), *Poetry Matters* (Peterloo Poets), *Poetry Review, Poetry Wales, Spare Rib, Sunk Island Review, Ti (Pi) International Poetry Review*, and *Wordworks* (Bloodaxe Books/Tyne Tees Television, 1992).

I would also like to thank Kathryn Perry, Wendy Young, Fred D'Aguiar, Carol Ann Duffy, Frances Anne Soloman and Helen and John Kay for their encouragement and criticism. And a special thank you to Louise Roscoe for her fine ear and sharp eye.

The cover photograph is reproduced by kind permission of CNRI/Science Photo Library. It shows a false-colour light micrograph of human chromosomes, obtained by amniocentesis.

# Contents

# THE ADOPTION PAPERS

In *The Adoption Papers* sequence, the voices of the three speakers are distinguished typographically:

DAUGHTER:            Palatino typeface *(as rest of book)*

ADOPTIVE MOTHER:     Gill typeface

BIRTH MOTHER:        Bodoni typeface

# THE ADOPTION PAPERS

I always wanted to give birth
do that incredible natural thing
that women do – I nearly broke down
when I heard we couldn't,
and then my man said
well there's always adoption
(we didn't have test tubes and the rest then)
even in the early sixties there was
something scandalous about adopting,
telling the world your secret failure
bringing up an alien child,
who knew what it would turn out to be


I was pulled out with forceps
left a gash down my left cheek
four months inside a glass cot
but she came faithful
from Glasgow to Edinburgh
and peered through the glass
I must have felt somebody willing me to survive;
she would not pick another baby


I still have the baby photograph
I keep it in my bottom drawer

She is twenty-six today
my hair is grey

The skin around my neck is wrinkling
does she imagine me this way

# PART ONE: 1961-1962

## Chapter 1: The Seed

I never thought it would be quicker
than walking down the mainstreet

I want to stand in front of the mirror
swollen bellied so swollen bellied

The time, the exact time
for that particular seed to be singled out

I want to lie on my back at night
I want to pee all the time

amongst all others
like choosing a dancing partner

I crave discomfort like some women
crave chocolate or earth or liver

Now these slow weeks on
I can't stop going over and over

I can't believe I've tried for five years
for something that could take five minutes

It only took a split second
not a minute or more.

I want the pain
the tearing searing pain

I want my waters to break
like Noah's flood

I want to push and push
and scream and scream.

When I was sure I wrote a short note
six weeks later – a short letter

He was sorry; we should have known better
He couldn't leave Nigeria.

I missed him, silly things
his sudden high laugh,

His eyes intense as whirlwind
the music he played me

## Chapter 2: The Original Birth Certificate

I say to the man at the desk
I'd like my original birth certificate
Do you have any idea what your name was?
Close, close he laughs. *Well what was it?*

So slow as torture he discloses bit by bit
my mother's name, my original name
the hospital I was born in, the time I came.

Outside Edinburgh is soaked in sunshine
I talk to myself walking past the castle.
So, so, so, I was a midnight baby after all.

I am nineteen
my whole life is changing

On the first night
I see her shuttered eyes in my dreams

I cannot pretend she's never been
my stitches pull and threaten to snap

my own body a witness
leaking blood to sheets, milk to shirts


On the second night
I'll suffocate her with a feather pillow

Bury her under a weeping willow
Or take her far out to sea

and watch her tiny eight-pound body
sink to shells and reshape herself.

So much the better than her body
encased in glass like a museum piece


On the third night
I toss I did not go through these months

for you to die on me now
on the third night I lie

willing life into her
breathing air all the way down the corridor

to the glass cot
I push my nipples through

## Chapter 3: The Waiting Lists

The first agency we went to
didn't want us on their lists,
we didn't live close enough to a church
nor were we church-goers
(though we kept quiet about being communists).
The second told us
we weren't high enough earners.
The third liked us
but they had a five-year waiting list.
I spent six months trying not to look
at swings nor the front of supermarket trolleys,
not to think this kid I've wanted could be five.
The fourth agency was full up.
The fifth said yes but again no babies.
Just as we were going out the door
I said oh you know we don't mind the colour.
Just like that, the waiting was over.

This morning a slim manilla envelope arrives
postmarked Edinburgh: one piece of paper
I have now been able to look up your microfiche
(as this is all the records kept nowadays).
From your mother's letters, the following information:
Your mother was nineteen when she had you.
You weighed eight pounds four ounces.
She liked hockey. She worked in Aberdeen
as a waitress. She was five foot eight inches.

I thought I'd hid everything
that there wasnie wan
giveaway sign left

I put Marx Engels Lenin (no Trotsky)
in the airing cupboard – she'll no be
checking out the towels surely

All the copies of the *Daily Worker*
I shoved under the sofa
the dove of peace I took down from the loo

A poster of Paul Robeson
saying give him his passport
I took down from the kitchen

I left a bust of Burns
my detective stories
and the Complete Works of Shelley

She comes at 11.30 exactly.
I pour her coffee
from my new Hungarian set

And foolishly pray she willnae
ask its origins – honestly
this baby is going to my head.

She crosses her legs on the sofa
I fancy I hear the *Daily Workers*
rustle underneath her

Well she says, you have an interesting home
She sees my eyebrows rise.
It's different she qualifies.

Hell and I've spent all morning
trying to look ordinary
– a lovely home for the baby.

She buttons her coat all smiles
I'm thinking
I'm on the home run

But just as we get to the last post
her eye catches at the same times as mine
a red ribbon with twenty world peace badges

Clear as a hammer and sickle
on the wall.
Oh, she says are you against nuclear weapons?

To Hell with this. Baby or no baby.
Yes I says. Yes yes yes.
I'd like this baby to live in a nuclear free world.

Oh. Her eyes light up.
I'm all for peace myself she says,
and sits down for another cup of coffee.

## Chapter 4: Baby Lazarus

Land moves like driven cattle
My eyes snatch pieces of news
headlines strung out on a line:
MOTHER DROWNS BABY IN THE CLYDE

November

The social worker phoned,
our baby is a girl but not healthy
she won't pass the doctor's test
until she's well. The adoption papers
can't be signed. I put the phone down.
I felt all hot. Don't get overwrought.
What does she expect? I'm not a mother
until I've signed that piece of paper.

The rhythm of the train carries me
over the frigid earth
the constant chug a comforter
a rocking cradle.

16

Maybe the words lie
across my forehead
headline in thin ink
MOTHER GIVES BABY AWAY


December

We drove through to Edinburgh,
I was that excited the forty miles
seemed a lifetime. What do you think she'll
look like? I don't know my man says. I could tell
he was as nervous as me. On the way back his face
was one long smile even although
he didn't get inside. Only me.
I wore a mask but she didn't seem to mind
I told her *any day now my darling any day.*

Nobody would ever guess.
I had no other choice
Anyway it's best for her,
My name signed on a dotted line.


March

Our baby has passed.
We can pick her up in two days.
Two days for Christ's sake,
could they not have given us a bit more notice?


Land moves like driven cattle

I must stop it. Put it out my mind.
There is no use going over and over.
I'm glad she's got a home to go to.
This sandwich is plastic.

I forgot to put sugar in the flask.
The man across the table keeps staring.
I should have brought another book –
all this character does is kiss and say sorry


go and come back,
we are all foolish with trust.
I used to like winter
the empty spaces, the fresh air.


When I got home
I went out into the garden –
the frost bit my old brown boots –
and dug a hole the size of my baby
and buried the clothes I'd bought anyway.
A week later I stood at my window
and saw the ground move and swell
the promise of a crop,
that's when she started crying.
I gave her a service then, sang
Ye banks and braes, planted
a bush of roses, read the Book of Job,
cursed myself digging a pit for my baby
sprinkling ash from the grate.
Late that same night
she came in by the window,
my baby Lazarus
and suckled at my breast.

## Chapter 5: The Tweed Hat Dream

Today I ring the counselling agency in Edinburgh.
Can you start to trace through marriage certificates?
*It will take three weeks what do you expect from it.*
If she wants to meet me that's fine if she doesn't
that is also fine

This morning the counselling woman rings
she's found someone who might be her
she's not sure; do I know my grandmother's name?
*Pity.* She'll be in touch, not sure when.


Her mother just turns up at the door
with a tweed hat on. I thinks
she doesn't suit tweed, she's too young.
In all these months I've never put a face to her
that looks like my daughter – so picture me
when I see those lips. She looks a dead spit
except of course she's white; lightning white.
She says in her soft Highland voice
*can you let me see her? Can you?*
What could I do? She comes in swift
as wind in a storm, rushes up the stairs
as if she knows the house already,
picks up my baby and strokes her cheeks endlessly
till I get tired and say, I'll be downstairs.

I put the kettle on, maybe
hot tea will redden those white cheeks,
arrange a plate of biscuits which keep
sliding onto the floor.
She's been up there helluva long.
I don't know where the thought comes from
but suddenly I'm pounding the stairs
like thunder. Her tweed hat
is in the cot. That is all.

That night I turn it through till dawn
a few genes, blood, a birth.
All this bother, certificates, papers.
It is all so long ago. Does it matter?
Now I come from her,
the mother who stole my milk teeth
ate the digestive left for Santa

## Chapter 6: The Telling Part

Ma mammy bot me oot a shop
Ma mammy says I was a luvly baby

Ma mammy picked me (I wiz the best)
your mammy had to take you (she'd no choice)

Ma mammy says she's no really ma mammy
(just kid on)

It's a bit like a part you've rehearsed so well
you can't play it on the opening night
She says my real mammy is away far away
Mammy why aren't you and me the same colour
But I love my mammy whether she's real or no
My heart started rat tat tat like a tin drum
all the words took off to another planet
Why


But I love ma mammy whether she's real or no

I could hear the upset in her voice
I says *I'm not your real mother,*
though Christ knows why I said that,
If I'm not who is, but all my planned speech
went out the window

She took me when I'd nowhere to go
my mammy is the best mammy in the world OK.

After mammy telt me she wisnae my real mammy
I was scared to death she was gonnie melt
or something or mibbe disappear in the dead
of night and somebody would say she wis a fairy
godmother. So the next morning I felt her skin
to check it was flesh, but mibbe it was just
a good imitation. How could I tell if my mammy
was a dummy with a voice spoken by someone else?
So I searches the whole house for clues
but I never found nothing. Anyhow a day after
I got my guinea pig and forgot all about it.

I always believed in the telling anyhow.
You can't keep something like that secret
I wanted her to think of her other mother
out there, thinking that child I had will be
seven today eight today all the way up to
god knows when. I told my daughter –
I bet your mother's never missed your birthday,
how could she?


Mammy's face is cherries.
She is stirring the big pot of mutton soup
singing *I gave my love a cherry*
*it had no stone.*
I am up to her apron.
I jump onto her feet and grab her legs
like a huge pair of trousers,
she walks round the kitchen lifting me up.

Suddenly I fall off her feet.
And mammy falls to the floor.
She won't stop the song
*I gave my love a chicken it had no bone.*
I run next door for help.
When me and Uncle Alec come back
Mammy's skin is toffee stuck to the floor.
And her bones are all scattered like toys.


22

Now when people say 'ah but
it's not like having your own child though is it',
I say of course it is, what else is it?
she's my child, I have told her stories
wept at her losses, laughed at her pleasures,
she is mine.

I was always the first to hear her in the night
all this umbilical knot business is nonsense
– the men can afford deeper sleeps that's all.
I listened to hear her talk,
and when she did I heard my voice under hers
and now some of her mannerisms crack me up


Me and my best pal
don't have Donny Osmond or David Cassidy
on our walls and we don't wear Starsky and Hutch
jumpers either. Round at her house we put on
the old record player and mime to Pearl Bailey
Tired of the life I lead, tired of the blues I breed
and Bessie Smith I can't do without my kitchen man.
Then we practise ballroom dancing giggling,
everyone thinks we're dead old-fashioned.

# Chapter 7: Black Bottom

Maybe that's why I don't like
all this talk about her being black,
I brought her up as my own
as I would any other child
colour matters to the nutters;
but she says my daughter says
it matters to her

I suppose there would have been things
I couldn't understand with any child,
we knew she was coloured.
They told us they had no babies at first
and I chanced it didn't matter what colour it was
and they said *oh well are you sure
in that case we have a baby for you* –
to think she wasn't even thought of as a baby,
my baby, my baby

I chase his *Sambo Sambo* all the way from the school gate.
A fistful of anorak – What did you call me? Say that again.
*Sam-bo.* He plays the word like a bouncing ball
but his eyes move fast as ping pong.
I shove him up against the wall,
say that again you wee shite. *Sambo, sambo,* he's crying now

I knee him in the balls. What was that?
My fist is steel; I punch and punch his gut.
Sorry I didn't hear you? His tears drip like wax.
*Nothing* he heaves *I didn't say nothing.*
I let him go. He is a rat running. He turns
and shouts *Dirty Darkie* I chase him again.
Blonde hairs in my hand. Excuse me!
This teacher from primary 7 stops us.
Names? I'll report you to the headmaster tomorrow.
But Miss. Save it for Mr Thompson she says

My teacher's face cracks into a thin smile
Her long nails scratch the note well well
I see you were fighting yesterday, again.
In a few years time you'll be a juvenile delinquent.
Do you know what that is? Look it up in the dictionary.
She spells each letter with slow pleasure.
Read it out to the class.
Thug. Vandal. Hooligan. Speak up. Have you lost your tongue?

To be honest I hardly ever think about it
except if something happens, you know
daft talk about darkies. Racialism.
Mothers ringing my bell with their kids
crying *You tell. You tell. You tell.*
– *No.* You tell your little girl to stop calling
my little girl names and I'll tell my little girl
to stop giving your little girl a doing.

We're practising for the school show
I'm trying to do the Cha Cha and the Black Bottom
but I can't get the steps right
my right foot's left and my left foot's right
my teacher shouts from the bottom
of the class Come on, show

us what you can do I thought
you people had it in your blood.
My skin is hot as burning coal
like that time she said Darkies are like coal
in front of the whole class – my blood
what does she mean? I thought

she'd stopped all that after the last time
my dad talked to her on parents' night
the other kids are all right till she starts;
my feet step out of time, my heart starts
to miss beats like when I can't sleep at night –
*What Is In My Blood?* The bell rings, it is time.

Sometimes it is hard to know what to say
that will comfort. Us two in the armchair;
me holding her breath, 'they're ignorant
let's have some tea and cake, forget them'.


Maybe it's really Bette Davis I want
to be the good twin or even better the bad
one or a nanny who drowns a baby in a bath.
I'm not sure maybe I'd prefer Katharine
Hepburn tossing my red hair, having a hot
temper. I says to my teacher Can't I be
Elizabeth Taylor, drunk and fat and she
just laughed, not much chance of that.
I went for an audition for *The Prime
of Miss Jean Brodie*. I didn't get a part
even thought I've been acting longer
than Beverley Innes. So I have. Honest.


Olubayo was the colour of peat
when we walked out heads turned
like horses, folk stood like trees
their eyes fixed on us – it made me
burn, that hot glare; my hand
would sweat down to his bone.
Finally, alone, we'd melt
nothing, nothing would matter


He never saw her. I looked for him in her;
for a second it was as if he was there
in that glass cot looking back through her.


On my bedroom wall is a big poster
of Angela Davis who is in prison
right now for nothing at all
except she wouldn't put up with stuff.
My mum says she is *only* 26
which seems really old to me
but my mum says it is young

just imagine, she says, being on
America's Ten Most Wanted People's List at 26!
I can't.
Angela Davis is the only female person
I've seen (except for a nurse on TV)
who looks like me. She had big hair like mine
that grows out instead of down.
My mum says it's called an *Afro*.
If I could be as brave as her when I get older
I'll be OK.
Last night I kissed her goodnight again
and wondered if she could feel the kisses
in prison all the way from Scotland.
Her skin is the same too you know.
I can see my skin is that colour
but most of the time I forget,
so sometimes when I look in the mirror
I give myself a bit of a shock
and say to myself *Do you really look like this?*
as if I'm somebody else. I wonder if she does that.

I don't believe she killed anybody.
It is all a load of phoney lies.
My dad says it's a set up.
I asked him if she'll get the electric chair
like them Roseberries he was telling me about.
No he says the world is on her side.
Well how come she's in there then I thinks.
I worry she's going to get the chair.
I worry she's worrying about the chair.
My dad says she'll be putting on a brave face.
He brought me a badge home which I wore
to school. It says FREE ANGELA DAVIS.
And all my pals says 'Who's she?'

# PART THREE: 1980-1990

## Chapter 8: Generations

The sun went out just like that
almost as if it had never been,
hard to imagine now the way it fell
on treetops, thatched roofs, people's faces.
Suddenly the trees lost their nerves
and the grass passed the wind on
blade to blade, fast as gossip

Years later, the voices still come close
especially in dreams, not distant echoes
loud – a pneumatic drill – deeper and deeper still.
I lived the scandal, wore it casual
as a summer's dress, Jesus sandals.
All but the softest whisper:
*she's lost an awful lot of weight.*

Now my secret is the hush of heavy curtains drawn.
I dread strange handwriting
sometimes jump when the phone rings,
she is all of nineteen and legally able.
At night I lie practising my lines
but 'sorry' never seems large enough
nor 'I can't see you, yes, I'll send a photograph.'


I was pulled out with forceps
left a gash down my left cheek
four months inside a glass cot
but
she came faithful from Glasgow to Edinburgh
and peered through the glass
she would not pick another baby.

I don't know what diseases
come down my line;
when dentist and doctors ask
the old blood questions about family runnings
I tell them: I have no nose or mouth or eyes
to match, no spitting image or dead cert,
my face watches itself in the glass.

I have my parents who are not of the same tree
and you keep trying to make it matter,
the blood, the tie, the passing down
generations.
We all have our contradictions,
the ones with the mother's nose and father's eyes
have them;
the blood does not bind confusion,
yet I confess to my contradiction
I want to know my blood.

I know my blood.
It is dark ruby red and comes
regular and I use Lillets.
I know my blood when I cut my finger.
I know what my blood looks like.

It is the well, the womb, the fucking seed.
Here, I am far enough away to wonder –
what were their faces like
who were my grandmothers
what were the days like
passed in Scotland
the land I come from
the soil in my blood.

Put it this way:
I know she thinks of me often
when the light shows its face
or the dark skulks behind hills,
she conjures me up or I just appear

when I take the notion, my slippers
are silent and I walk through doors.

She's lying in bed; I wake her up
a pinch on her cheek is enough,
then I make her think of me for hours.
The best thing I can steal is sleep.
I get right under the duvet and murmur
*you'll never really know your mother.*
I know who she thinks I am – she's made a blunder.

She is faceless
She has no nose
She is five foot eight inches tall
She likes hockey best
She is twenty-six today
She was a waitress
My hair is grey
She wears no particular dress
The skin around my neck is wrinkling
Does she imagine me this way?
Lately I make pictures of her
But I can see the smallness
She is tall and slim
of her hands, Yes
Her hair is loose curls
an opal stone on her middle finger
I reach out to catch her
Does she talk broad Glasgow?
But no matter how fast
Maybe they moved years ago
I run after
She is faceless, she never
weeps. She has neither eyes nor
fine boned cheeks

Once would be enough,
just to listen to her voice
watch the way she moves her hands
when she talks.

## Chapter 9: The Phone Call

I have had my grandmother's Highland number
for four months now burning a hole in my filofax.

Something this morning gives me courage
to close the kitchen door and dial.

My grandmother's voice sounds much younger
'I used to work ages ago with your daughter

Elizabeth, do you have her present address?'
*Sorry*, she says, *No, but one of the girls*

*will have it*. She gives me another Highland number
wishing me luck. *What did you say your name was?*

Thirty minutes later my mother's sister
asks lots of questions – *Where did you work?*

*How long ago was that? What age are you?*
*Forty* I lie. *For a minute I thought…*

*But if you're forty, you can't be.*
I know she knows. The game's a bogey.

Actually I'm 26. *I thought so love.*
*I thought it was you. Mam knew too.*

*She just rang to warn me you'd ring.*
*How are you? How's your life been?*

*I'll give her yours. She'll write.*
*I'm sure you understand.* I do. I do.

Now she's gone. I get phone calls regularly.
It's not that I think I'm losing out but
I've surprised myself just the same;
I've had to stop myself saying, 'drop
it, you'll get hurt'. I do worry
of course I do, but it's me that's hurt.
Tonight I cried watching bloody Adam
Carrington discover he's not a Carrington
any more. Daft. Getting myself into a tizzy.


## Chapter 10: The Meeting Dream


*If I picture it like this it hurts less*
We are both shy
though our eyes are not,
they pierce below skin.
We are not as we imagined:
I am smaller, fatter, darker
**I am taller, thinner**
and I'd always imagined her hair dark brown
not grey. I can see my chin in hers
that is all, though no doubt
my mum will say, when she looks at the photo,
**she's your double she really is.**

There is no sentiment in this living-room,
a plain wood table and a few books.
We don't cuddle or even shake hands
though we smile sudden as a fire blazing
then die down.
Her hands play with her wedding-ring,
I've started smoking again.

We don't ask big questions even later by the shore.
We walk slow, tentative as crabs
No, so what have you been doing the past 26 years.
Just what are you working at, stuff like that.


Ages later I pick up a speckled stone
and hurl it into the sea,
is this how you imagined it to be?
I never imagined it.
Oh. I hear the muffled splash.
It would have driven me mad imagining,
26 years is a long time.


Inside once more I sip hot tea
notice one wood-framed photo.
The air is as old as the sea.
I stare at her chin till she makes me look down.
Her hands are awkward as rocks.
My eyes are stones washed over and over.

*If I picture it like this it hurts less*

One dream cuts another open like a gutted fish
nothing is what it was;
she is too many imaginings to be flesh and blood.
There is nothing left to say.
Neither of us mentions meeting again.

When I'm by myself watching the box
it's surprising how often it crops
up; that he or she didn't know anything about it
and now who is he or she really
do they love who they thought they loved
et cetera. You've got the picture.
Mine knew. As soon as possible
I always told her, if you ever want to,
I won't mind. I wasn't trying to be big
about it – if that was me, that's how I'd be.
Curiosity. It's natural. Origins.
That kind of thing. See me and her
there is no mother and daughter more similar.
We're on the wavelength so we are.
Right away I know if she's upset.
And vice versa. Closer than blood.
Thicker than water. Me and my daughter.


I wrapped up well and went out before
The birds began their ritual blether

I wrapped her up in purple wrapping paper
And threw her down the old well near here.
There was no sound, it's no longer
In use – years – she's been in my drawer
Faded now, she's not a baby any more

Still pitch dark. It didn't matter.
I know every bend. I've no more terror.
Going home, the light spilled like water.


Her sister said she'd write me a letter.
In the morning I'm awake with the birds
waiting for the crash of the letter box
then the soft thud of words on the matt.
I lie there, duvet round my shoulders
fantasising the colour of her paper
whether she'll underline First Class
or have a large circle over her 'i's.

# SEVERE GALE 8

# Severe Gale 8

## NHS

There was no bread; he painted the sky
in oils – the clouds flushed with his passion
the trees sang like it was going out of fashion
and the wind waltzed with Matilda.

They had reached that decade in Britain –
people lined up against the walls,
mouths wide open, gold fillings pinched.

Those still breathing air and not on BUPA
were charged 10 new pence for three minutes
Those with sick children  and not on BUPA
had to make their own tiny umbrellas
for the holes in their hearts,
or wait perhaps one year
in the same white corridor
for that rare breed a doctor
who was by now almost a dinosaur.

## ££££

There was no bread so she told a story
until the story told another story
until all the People gathered eating
fiction like hot French bread, melted butter.

This was the decade when people
were given ansamachines for falling into debt,
when between them they owed £47 billion.
Bankers sat counting the numbers
all this gold from plastic –
They sang their tune at the Stock Exchange,

It went Tra la la la la la laughing.

One day when the wind was waltzing
so fast it stole people's hats
and punched dustbins in the gut
the people gathered to burn their plastic.
The smell was so strong it made them collectively faint.
A smart dressed man from Natwest
and another from the Midland
arrived with masks and put new pieces of plastic
in their pockets whilst they slept.


*Cardboard*

There was no bread; she collected jet
and shaped seagulls, butterflies, orchids
people wore round their necks or in ears
which heard her music her fantasy in C.

This was the decade when most lived
in cardboard cities and towns except
those with two massive stone houses.
It had come to this when Poll Tax
arrived that winter of the second hurricane,
sweeping the roofs of their old houses off
forcing mothers to first throw their children
out into the wind and watch them rise
over the odd remaining tree, past the tower block.


*The Pound*

There was no bread; she made a sculpture
using the metal of the cars, the blood of the dead
the odd relic of a brick from a house
some teeth that had been missed by the Snatchers.

This was the decade when every cardboard city
was so jam-packed that strangers
recognised each other's smells.

That winter all of the cars were taken
by the huge metal lobster and laid

out like bodies in a graveyard.
The money owed at the pound mounted
a tenner a day on top of the 75.
Some people owed  thousands.
Some sat in their cars and died
listening to *Black Box Remix* or *Desert Island Discs*.


### The Third Hurricane

The wind was revolutionary;
ducks and gulls and Canadian geese
levitated to catch flying pieces of bread.
Small children flew higher than hawks,
their fat little bodies buffeted by Galeforce 8
moving along at 95 mph.

Adults stood rooted
like the trees used to be,
their arms waving in the wind.

The children flew to Nicaragua Libre
to the Soviet Union, to South Africa
just in time to see a man who no longer
looked like his picture get released;
after 27 years they sang the anthem
they learned on the way there.

They brought him a turtle dove
and took their leave.

When they returned the wind stopped
and they landed soft as feathers –
some people were dead, the rest were marching
all the way down to all the way down to

la la la la laughing.

## It used to excite me even

standing at my bedroom window, breath on the glass
the dark arms of the cherry blossom
gesticulating madly; roofs like hats
blown off – best, the school one next morning.
Candles at home, toast from the coal fire.
Nightime again and that soft hysterical laughter
her and her mates gathering for another party,
standing at my bedroom window, breath on the glass.

Now it steals my sleep and whispers warnings,
finally when I do fall off there's glass flying.
Next morning – wooden corpses on the street.
The world is all strange and unbelievable.
I tiptoe over the devastation to buy some milk.
The kettle whistles as I lipread global warming;
I imagine a person with 90 degree burns all over.
The hot tea starts to brew its own storm. I can't scream.

# My Grandmother's Houses

1

She is on the second floor of a tenement
From her front room window you see the cemetery

Her bedroom is my favourite: newspapers
dating back to the War covering every present
she's ever got since the War. What's the point
in buying her anything my mother moans.
Does she use it. Does she even look at it.
I spend hours unwrapping and wrapping endless
tablecloths, napkins, perfume, bath salts,
stories of things I can't understand, words
like conscientious objector. At night I climb
over all the newspaper parcels to get to bed,
harder than the school's obstacle course. High up
in her bed all the print merges together.

When she gets the letter she is hopping mad.
What does she want with anything modern,
a shiny new pin? Here is home.
The sideboard solid as a coffin.
The newsagents next door which sells
hazelnut toffees and her *Daily Record*.
Chewing for ages over the front page,
her toffees sticking to her false teeth.

2

The new house is called a high rise.
I play in the lift all the way up to 24.
Once I get stuck for a whole hour.
From her window you see noisy kids
playing hopscotch or home.
She  makes endless pots of vegetable soup,
a big bit of hoch floating inside like a fish

Till finally she gets to like the hot
running water in her own bathroom
the wall-to-wall foam-backed carpet
the parcels locked in her air-raid shelter.

40

But she still doesn't settle down;
even at 70 she cleans people's houses
for ten bob and goes to church on Sundays,
dragging me along to the strange place where the air
is trapped and ghosts sit at the altar.
My parents do not believe. It is down to her.
A couple of prayers. A hymn or two.
Threepenny bit in the collection hat.
A flock of women in coats and fussy hats
flapping over me like missionaries, and that is that,
until the next time God grabs me in Glasgow with Gran.


3

By the time I am seven we are almost the same height.
She still walks faster, rushing me down the High Street
till we get to her cleaning house. The hall is huge.
Rooms lead off like an octopus's arms.
I sit in a room with a grand piano, top open –
a one-winged creature, whilst my gran polishes
for hours. Finally bored I start to pick some notes
oh can you wash a sailor's shirt oh can you wash and clean
till my gran comes running, duster in hand.
I told you don't touch anything. The woman comes too;
the posh one all smiles that make goosepimples
run up my arms. Would you like to sing me a song?
Someone's crying my Lord Kumbaya. Lovely, she says,
beautiful child, skin the colour of café au lait.
'Café oh what? Hope she's not being any bother.'
Not at all. Not at all. You just get back to your work.
On the way back to her high rise I see her
like the hunchback of Notre Dame. Everytime I crouch
over a comic she slaps me. Sit up straight.

She is on the ground floor of a high rise.
From her living-room you see ambulances,
screaming their way to the Royal Infirmary.

# Summer Storm, Capolona

I choose to ignore my instinct for the sky's
warning – the way each light flicks out
the strange smell in the air, a herbal brew;
you are crying to go out and the four walls
of the villa are coming in like a fast tide.

The poppies in the wheat have darkened to dried
blood; the air sharpens itself, a scythe,
you are giggling inside your window hood
when the first raindrops fall like cherries;
this is our last chance to see the grape vines.

Tomorrow we will be up in the air.
I walk faster. Strangers watch from square
windows. Am I crazy? Laughter like lightning.
The poppies in the wheat, whirling, twirling
to the tribal drum roll up there.

I start to run; hands tight on the buggy.
The cherries have turned into stones.
I am being punished in that old public way.
I curse myself, count in my head
ask each tree I chase to save us.

Didn't somebody say more people die
of lightning than aeroplane crashes.
Never hide under a tree. It might never pass.
A man peers down from a farmhouse on a hill.
Bambino? He shouts Venga venga, are you mad?

Inside the poverty is one fish multiplied.
We are offered madeira cake meant for special
and strong coffee for me.You pull the stubble
on the old man's face. The woman irons shirts
that have been washed a million times.

I have about ten Italian words.
That is your son. He was drowned.
Five years ago? I don't know how to say
I'm sorry. You ask me where my husband is.
I tell you I haven't got one. You indicate *pity*.

We are safe in a small madeira cake house.
Through the window, light rises like Lazarus.
The rain is soft and harmless once again,
magic. We walk out, after you say Ciaou
ten times, with their umbrella just in case.

They both stand waving. Come back when
the bambino is – they slice the air
higher and higher. Yes I say, but I am
coming back much sooner with an
umbrella and another madeira cake.

## Pounding Rain

News of us spreads like a storm.
The top of our town to the bottom.
We stand behind curtains
parted like hoods; watch each other's eyes.

We talk of moving to the west end,
this bit has always been a shoe box
tied with string; but then again
your father still lives in that house
where we warmed up spaghetti bolognese
in lunch hours and danced to Louis Armstrong,
his gramophone loud as our two heart beats
going boom diddy boom diddy boom.

Did you know then? I started dating Davy;
when I bumped into you I'd just say Hi.
I tucked his photo booth smile into my satchel
brought him out for my pals in the intervals.

A while later I heard you married Trevor Campbell.
Each night I walked into the school dinner hall
stark naked, till I woke to Miss, Miss Miss
every minute. Then, I bumped into you at the Cross.

You haven't changed you said; that reassurance.
Nor you; your laugh still crosses the street.
I trace you back, beaming , till –
Why don't you come round, Trevor would love it.

He wasn't in. I don't know how it happened.
We didn't bother with a string of do you remembers.
I ran my fingers through the beads in your hair.
Your hair's nice I said stupidly, nice, suits you.

We sat and stared till our eyes filled
like a glass of wine. I did it, the thing
I'd dreamt a million times. I undressed you
slowly, each item of clothing fell
with a sigh. I stroked your silk skin
until we were back in the Campsies, running
down the hills in the pounding rain,
screaming and laughing; soaked right through.

# In the Seventh Year
*(for Louise)*


Our sea is still mysterious as morning mist
its flapping arms stretched out for dry sand
its running heels sliding over pebbles
when the sun dives in at night

We are turquoise and clear some days
still as breeze; others stormy like stones
you are in deep stroking my bones
my love an ache, the early light

spreading the water
seven years seven years I repeat
over and over
clasping this timeless, this changing thing.

# Photo in the Locket

*(for Louise)*

I

There are things I don't tell her
private things, a garnet necklace
slipped between black silk and cotton.
My new friend gives me an African name
writes letters often; once she sent one
with a spicy bun, a can of black grape
and an old photo of her and her sister –
two black girls side by side
in identical white lace dresses,
big bows on their nappy (a word
I've just learnt) hair and ankle socks.
So clean. Black people are hot on hygiene.
White people sleep with cats and dogs.

*I don't talk about these things.*
*My past is locked in a travelling trunk.*
*Inside: Sabena, my nanny, my mother*
*her long black fingers shine*
*like reefs lit by moonlight;*
*my house; the swimming pool;*
*my old white public school.*
*I'm ashamed. I didn't think much.*
*Sometimes I see the black man's face*
*at the window, coming to get us.*

My mother is white. My father is white.
My lover is white. At night we lie
like spoons breathing the same cold air
inside the room with two outside walls.
We snuggle under blankets, sometimes
turn in unison our bodies all
mixed up.
We can only meet here in bed –
my fingers inside her high tide,
she making a rivulet run through me
in a rush, a gush till we are both
beached up.

*When my family first met her*
*they thought I was undoing my past*
*through her. It's not like that.*
*I love her. Not like I loved Sabena.*
*I love lying next to her*
*the dark of her skin, the pale of mine.*
*Sometimes I want to tell her,*
*if you knew what it was really like:*
*servants living in corrugated huts outside*
*no electricity, no running water*
*you wouldn't be lying here kissing my breasts.*

*I keep it hidden. Locked – a photo*
*inside a locket that never opens*

In the morning I wake before you
the pale winter light peeps through
our skin; side by side, in sharp relief.
Something I've been reading in *Midnight Birds*
makes me feel like Judas;
I get up make toast and tea.

I am five years old again
looking out this kitchen window.
Somebody turns the palm of my hand
up and asks why it isn't black.
Is your bottom black someone sniggers.
Then they all laugh. I put loose leaves
in the tea-pot. Let them brew.
Last night we talked into the small
hours again. You said they used to call
you specky. The toast burns.
I pull it out furious. It is not
the same. It is not the same.
I don't want to play it out on you.
You get up for breakfast:
'I'm always making the fucking toast',
before you rub the sleep out of your eyes.

*Yesterday I said a terrible thing.*
*My tongue is full of old ideas.*
*Sometimes they slip like falling rocks.*

*Warning. Landslide. I can't repeat it.*
*She'll repeat it for me.*
*Often. So that I don't forget.*

*This is the nightmare: the soft laughter*
*then this sudden storm. I don't know where*
*we go wrong. I am all that. True.*
*I lived it. Now I live with her. Together.*
*Not as servant and Madam. No.*
*Not like that, I don't believe her.*
*As lovers, as lovers, as lovers.*
*Words chase me like bullets overhead.*
*Kaffir. Wog. Kaffir. Wog.*
*Between tight teeth I whisper.*

I hug say sorry let's go back
to bed. We're too young. This
is too heavy. I'd like to stop seeing
white like whitewash on hospital walls
like a blank projection screen;
black like onyx stones or moist earth.

What am I doing with you
if all I want is to make you
eat shit for your ancestors?

*It's better for her now down here*
*in London. Yet still with her friends*
*I shake a little when I'm pouring tea.*
*Waiting for discovery. They disapprove*
*I'm sure of the two of us together.*
*At clubs we separate for the evening,*
*come back together in bed much later,*
*where no eyes watch like marbles.*

*Tonight while she sleeps*
*I lie thinking of home.*
*I miss the land. The red dust roads.*
*The jacaranda tree, picking ripe avocados*
*or mangoes. I miss the words; the whole tutti.*
*I don't talk of this. Even memories*
*lead to trouble. Especially memories.*

*Which school. What house. Which friend.*
*We were brought up on different worlds:*
*she on mince and potatoes, drizzle, midges;*
*me on mealies, thunderstorms, chongalolas.*

II

Now I tell you almost everything.
Something shifted like sand
a while ago and the sea thrashed
out and in, carrying my secrets back
with the eventide. And my tongue
returned to the cave in my mouth.

You tell me when you were wee
you stood on a baby chick, squashed it,
how you felt it for years underfoot.
I tell you our rabbit Harvey
was strangled and buried in
our very own back garden.

Now, some of your memories are mine.
We move on. We don't forget.
We change not like amoebas
more like plants keeping the same stem.

*Now we are light years away.*
*Sometime ago I opened my trunk*
*and showed her a photo of Sabena.*
*Then it all came out. My strawberry dress.*
*The school assembly. Hot rain on dust.*
*Bit by bit we sat and picked till*
*I laughed and cried like some huge*
*waterfall – giggling and howling.*

# Dance of the Cherry Blossom

Both of us are getting worse
Neither knows who had it first

He thinks I gave it to him
I think he gave it to me

Nights chasing clues where
One memory runs into another like dye.

Both of us are getting worse
I know I'm wasting precious time

But who did he meet between
May 87 and March 89.

I feel his breath on my back
A slow climb into himself then out.

In the morning it all seems different
Neither knows who had it first

We eat breakfast together – newspapers
And silence except for the slow slurp of tea

This companionship is better than anything
He thinks I gave it to him.

By lunchtime we're fighting over some petty thing
He tells me I've lost my sense of humour

I tell him I'm not Glaswegian
You all think death is a joke

It's not funny. I'm dying for fuck's sake
I think he gave it to me.

Just think he says it's every couple's dream
I won't have to wait for you up there

I'll have you night after night – your glorious legs
Your strong hard belly, your kissable cheeks

I cry when he says things like that
My shoulders cave in, my breathing trapped

Do you think you have a corner on dying
You self-pitying wretch, pathetic queen.

He pushes me; we roll on the floor like whirlwind;
When we are done in, our lips find each other

We touch soft as breeze, caress the small parts
Rocking back and forth, his arms become mine

There's nothing outside but the noise of the wind
The cherry blossom's dance through the night.

## He Told Us He Wanted a Black Coffin
*(for Margaret McAllister)*

I phoned up the funeral director,
he said it would cost us a fortune
so we bought an ordinary pine one
painted it black matt like his furniture.
It looked smashing. He went out
like Charles Rennie Mackintosh –
a single bunch of white lilies on top.
None but Derek's flowers.

These past few days I can't stop thinking
how I wanted to take the abscess out
of his five year old mouth and put it in mine;
I wanted to fall off that wall in Greig Street;
the day I swore at Mrs Calder
for calling my son a poof in front of hers.
I always knew from when he was thirteen
and he cried when Gavin moved to Aberdeen.

No morphine no morphine no morphine
I want to be alive when I'm alive
dead when I'm dead know what I mean.
No first aid box to fetch,
No oil of cloves, no germolene
nothing, nothing – his hand in mine
his thumb tap tapping my palm
me saying you're all right son

Everything is all messed up.
The boy careening down the hill in the park
his sledge a huge pair of wings, scarf flying.
The man in my kitchen laughing at my bad jokes
(who'll laugh now?) The man in the hospital bed
the size of the boy; his face a person from Belsen.
The song he sang at the school concert
(what was it?) It doesn't seem that long ago.

# Lighthouse Wall

*(for Derek Hughes)*

Somewhere beyond the thin lighthouse wall
I can feel him pulling me; hard tug of a net.
I can see his face, laughing and wet, rising
out of the waves, the cold Atlantic sea,
that holiday. That was some holiday: sex maybe
three, four times a day. He's urging me on – why
wait, why bother hanging on

My body is cold. I call my nurse all the time.
I have a thing that I squeeze and it bleeps him.
He has a nice little bottom. I'd love to pinch it.
In the hours when I am lucid I am so aware
of my body shrinking. I imagine I might just disappear
into the white cotton. I hold onto the hands of friends.
They start to merge together

In the hours – what kind of hours would you call
these? More like years, epochs, centuries one day
and a split second blink if you miss it another day.
I try and follow the clock on the wall. The little hand.
The big hand. It's all pointless. I take my glasses off.
I put my glasses on. On and off on and off off and
the hands still the same time.

Today I'm having a blood transfusion. I am cold.
I ask the nurse for another blanket. He tells me
I am warm. I don't argue anymore. I haven't got
what? strength or time. I hate this though – self-pity:
I wrap it round myself like a velvet cloak or mist
from the sea; which sea would that be? The Black Sea.
The Red Sea. The North Sea.

I am running somewhere by the Baltic Sea; my body
is strong and fit. There is a space I can fall into.
There he is. His floral trunks. His forest legs.
It is quiet. I am full of awe. I kiss the salt
from his shoulders. He is rock hard. The long long
stretch of white sand is empty. The wind whips.
At last, I know this hand.

# Mummy and Donor and Deirdre

I went to school today.
I wore my new trainers, laces undone.
A nice boy called Tunde sat next to me.
In the playground he gave me a Monster
Munch; I gave him a bite of my apple.

We both went with him to school.
Took the day off. It was awful
long. It's happened so fast.
All day the hands of the clock moved in secret.
At last – his face at the gate. 'And then and then.'

He said my daddy is an underground man
What is your daddy? I said I don't have a daddy;
I have a mummy and a donor and a Deirdre.
Deirdre has hair the colour of that tree.
She helps people with no money.

I don't think we'll both go to parents' night.
I don't want things harder than they are.
I want to protect him from the names and stones.
I'd love it all to be different - Deirdre and me
in the PTA. Us on school holidays. No big deal.

Tunde said Do you know who your daddy is?
I said yes he's a friend of a friend of mummy's.
He has curly hair. He looks after animals.
I've got a picture. Come home and I'll show you.
We can play blockblusters. Don't you dare go away.

I was awful lucky. Third time with the syringe.
I didn't want Deirdre to do it with me.
I made myself all cosy. Lit a candle.
Had a body shop bath. Glass of Aqua Libre.
Wine's bad with sperm apparently.

I told Tunde some kids come from
their daddys using the penis; others from
their mummys using frozen sperm;
others because their mummys get the seed
put it in a syringe and put it in the vagina.

I wiped the tears from his face.
I kept saying don't cry, never mind.
Tunde won't play with him any more.
Are they dirty words, he asks me.
What am I supposed to say? Tell me.

Today Tunde and I said we won't tell
anybody else what we tell each other.
It will all be secret.I gave him a chocolate.
He gave me a Monster Munch.
Tunde has the same thing to eat everyday.

## Close Shave

The only time I forget is down the pit
right down in the belly of it,
my lamp shining like a third eye,
my breath short and fast like my wife's
when she's knitting. Snip snap.
I've tried to tell her as many times
as I've been down this mine. I can't
bring myself to, she'd tell our girls
most probably. It doesn't bear thinking.

Last night he shaved me again.
Close. Such an act of trust.
And he cut my hair; the scissors snip
snipped all night as I lay beside Ella
(Good job she's not that interested)
I like watching him sweep it up.
He holds the brush like a dancing partner,
short steps, fox trot: 4/4 time.
I knew from the first time, he did too

Our eyes met when he came
to the bit above my lip. 6 years ago.
We've only slept the night together twice:
once when my wife's sister died,
once when the brother-in-law committed suicide.
She left our daughters behind that time.
My nerves made me come too quick
but I liked sleeping in his smooth arms
till dawn. He was gone

Before they woke, giggling round breakfast.
He says nobody else can cut my curls.
I laughed loud for the first time since
God knows when. You're too vain man.
We kissed, I like his beard on my skin,
how can you be a barber with a beard
I said to him; it's my daughters that worry me.
Course I can never tell the boys down the pit.
When I'm down here I work fast so it hurts.

## Dressing Up
*(for Toby)*


My family's all so squalid
I'm trying to put it behind
me – real typical working class
Scottish: Da beats Ma drinks it off.
I couldn't stomach it, banging

doors, turning ma music up top
blast. I told ma ma years ago. She'd
rather I murdered somebody than
that. She wasn't joking either.
Nobody gets hurt, it's not for

the image even I'm just dead
childish. Mascara I like, rouge,
putting it on after powder.
I love wearing lots of layers.
Ma ma always dresses boring

No frills. See at Christmas I had
on black stockings Santa would kill
for and even Quentin Crisp would
look drab beside my beautiful
feather boa – bright fucking red.

Ma ma didn't touch her turkey
Finally she said What did I do
I know what they call you, transvite.
You look a bloody mess you do.
She had a black eye, a navy dress.

# I try my absolute best

I give my kids pure apple juice
(no sugar less acid than orange)
buy my baby soya milk formula
now she's off the breast
(non dairy, no cholesterol, good
for their little hearts – apparently
their arteries can harden before five
even). Water from the purifier.
Perrier if I'm feeling flush,
(they can always pretend it's lemonade).
Carob coated date bars. Cherry or banana.
And there's a shop down the street
that is selling organic vegetables
(no sprays, no chemicals).
Only to find the bloody English apples
are being sprayed with alar and are
carcinogenic; the soya beans are cooked
in aluminium pots which gives off deposits
in the brain; the cartridge in the purifier
collects things (like knickers if they're not changed).
Perrier's got Benzene in it which gives rats
cancer. Though I personally don't know any rat
that drinks Perrier, do you? And them
so-called Health Food Bars contain more sugar
than the average Mars Bar. What's the use
in calling anything organic when
the bloody soil's chock-a-block with lead?

I try my absolute best
drink decaff coffee to pipe me down
instead of hype me up only to find
out from my eldest daughter
that what they put the beans through
is worse for you than an ordinary Nescafé.

I'm back on Valium.
My kids are stuffing Monster Munch
and Mars Bars down them.

58

My youngest son even ate a hamburger yesterday.
It's driving me crazy.
I says it's your pocket money,
Do what you want with it.

# Death to Poll Tax

The doctor expects your mother to die
sometime during the night.


I am trying to get out at Piccadilly Circus
A man says sorry the exits are all closed.
Go back down. Leicester Square, the same thing happens.
I start to make the noise the tube makes
coming into the station. I imagine a fabulous
fire, licking its long lips through the tunnels
crossing the blue line into the red line into the black.

The first thing, at Tottenham Court Road, is a long line of
          masked men.
The second thing: a jagged star made from space
where the window was; two Hitachi TVs face down
on the street. The third thing is a man screaming
DEATH TO POLL TAX – a policeman punching him every time
he gets to Poll. Death to Poll THUD Tax. His voice is going
like the sirens in the distance.

The fourth thing: a man running, a child in each hand.
Come on Come on Come on. Hurry up.
I rush through the back streets. I have no map.
When I do arrive at the Cous Cous House
Kathryn is there: red lipstick, black silk top, neat bob.
I apologise for being late. We eat falafel.


You are in my kitchen waiting. What time I ask?
Eight o'clock you say. Sooner than they thought.

## Whilst Leila Sleeps

I am moving in the dead of night
packing things, turning out lights.
My fingers tie knots like fish nets.
I want to be in my mother's house
but she is all the way over

the other side of the world. Boxes;
I can't see out of the back window.
Leila is a bundle in her car seat.
Her small mouth hanging open.
Maybe it is not innocence after all

it could be the sleep of oblivion.
My headlights are  paranoic eyes
sweeping the streets for – what?
A split second before they appeared
I thought I was safe. What is that fear.

Does it have a name. They want my name.
Their smiles tighten my stomach.
I bite on my tongue, hard. Their faces.
I have no witness. They take my licence,
my papers. Now there is nothing left

but to go with the men in plain suits.
Leila stirs and opens her eyes wide.
I try and say something to soothe.
My voice is a house with the roof
blown off. What do I tell my daughter –

We are done for. There is a need to worry.
I cannot lie to her. The night dreams
my terror; a slow light tails the fast car;
Leila tugs at my coat. I whisper
her cradle song and she holds on.

# The Underground Baby Case

1

There was a couple of things
I wanted to remember

I was in the underground
on the Victoria Line, a mother
and her bags of digestives, disposables
disprin (possibly) got off, King's Cross
buggy first, then shopping,
then the doors closed.

We were in like sardines.

And I did a terrible thing.
I picked up the little boy and held him to my chest.
I picked up the little boy and held him to my chest.
I said There there mummy's here.
Don't you worry about a thing.
And then I started to sing the song sixpence,
and the song diamond ring.
Ali bali ali bali be ali bali ali bali be.
Next stop. I didn't get off.
The train flew like a plane.
Nobody noticed. Nobody said anything.

And he is a black boy
a beautiful black boy
skin like the sea at night
his lips are a blueberry pie.

2

He is my boy now. My boy.
In the morning we eat porridge together,
he drinks from the yellow cup I bought him.
When we go out in the big old fashioned pram
he pretends he is my washing.
At night I make him stories out of things

I'm trying to remember:
Little Red. Puff puff. King's Horses.
Her with the dreadful long hair.


### 3

Today when Peter had fallen asleep
in his little bed in my room,
comfier than away in the manger,
I slipped out and bought a newspaper
for the first time since the day his mother
gave him to me really, she must have wanted
me to have him – perhaps she planned it
for weeks, following me about,
picked me like you pick a disciple.


### 4

BABY KOFI MISSING 6 WEEKS

A black and white photo.
Is that how long it's been?
I've kept the picture for Peter
for when he's much older
and will understand.
I have not watched TV
for fear she will appear,
her long ropes of hair.


### 5

I would arrive at her house.
I would take my basket of fruit.
Inside: the empty plates at the table,
his toys scattered everywhere like memories.

I would climb up her hair.
And uncover her ear.
I would whisper Peter, Peter
is all right. Peter loves me.

And ever so gently I'd climb down
lock by lock, bone by bone,
trying to put her together again.


6

There was a couple of things
I wanted to remember
(must get nappies). I know
I've forgotten the date my baby was born
only the day in autumn she died;
in the black car on the 8th of October
the windscreen wipers waved like drowning hands,
the earth later, soft as a robin's breast,
eating my tiny baby up.